CORNERSTONES OF FREEDOM™

THE STATUE OF LIBERTY

BY DEBORAH KENT

CHILDREN'S PRESS®
An Imprint of Scholastic Inc.
New York   Toronto   London   Auckland   Sydney
Mexico City   New Delhi   Hong Kong
Danbury, Connecticut

BRINGING HISTORY to LIFE

Content Consultant
James Marten, PhD
Professor and Chair, History Department
Marquette University
Milwaukee, Wisconsin

Library of Congress Cataloging-in-Publication Data
Kent, Deborah.
  The Statue of Liberty/by Deborah Kent.
    p. cm.—(Cornerstones of freedom)
  Includes bibliographical references and index.
  ISBN-13: 978-0-531-23066-4 (lib. bdg.)   ISBN-10: 0-531-23066-X (lib. bdg.)
  ISBN-13: 978-0-531-28166-6 (pbk.)   ISBN-10: 0-531-28166-3 (pbk.)
  1. Statue of Liberty (New York, N.Y.)—Juvenile literature. 2. New
York (N.Y.)—Buildings, structures, etc.—Juvenile literature. I. Title. II.
Series.
  F128.64.L6K46 2012
  974.7—dc23   2011031125

Printed in the United States of America 113
SCHOLASTIC, CHILDREN'S PRESS, CORNERSTONES OF FREEDOM™,
and associated logos are trademarks and/or registered trademarks of
Scholastic Inc.

1 2 3 4 5 6 7 8 9 10 R 21 20 19 18 17 16 15 14 13 12

Photographs © 2012: AP Images: 42 (AIP), 7 (North Wind Picture Archives),
54 (Pictures, Inc.), 4 top, 55; Bridgeman Art Library/Private Collection/
The Stapleton Collection: 10, 56; Corbis Images/Julian Oliver Davidson: 5,
44; Getty Images/Hulton Archive: 15, 45; Granger Collection: 38 (Currier
and Ives), 50 (Edward Moran), 17, 57 (Jean Benner), 4 bottom, 24 (Rue
des Archives), 12, 14 bottom, 23, 30, 32, 49; Library of Congress: 36 (Albert
Fernique), 40 (Bain News Service), 39 (Centennial Photographic Co.), 19
(Civil War Glass Negative Collection), 47 (Harper's Monthly, 1885 July),
18 (Theodore Lilenthal), 6, 48, 57 bottom; National Park Service/Statue of
Liberty National Monument: 46 (American Museum of Immigration), 41;
North Wind Picture Archives: 20; Scholastic, Inc.: 64; Shutterstock, Inc.:
51 (Eniko Balogh), 16 (Fulcanelli), 26 (sculpies), 5 bottom, 29 (SVLuma),
cover (upthebanner), back cover (Yuri Arcurs); Superstock, Inc.: 14 top
(De Agostini), 22 (Clay Collection of Archiv for Kunst & Geschichte, Berlin),
28 (James Lemass), 2, 3, 37 (Musee Carnavalet, Paris/Universal Images
Group), 11, 35 (The Art Archive), 25; The Image Works: 33 (Fernique/Musée
Carnavalet/Roger-Viollet), 13 (Mary Evans Picture Library), 34 (ND/Roger-
Viollet), 27 (Roger-Viollet), 8 (The Print Collector/HIP).

Maps by XNR Productions, Inc.

Did you know that studying history can be fun?

BRING HISTORY TO LIFE by becoming a history investigator. Examine the evidence (primary and secondary source materials); cross-examine the people and witnesses. Take a look at what was happening at the time—but be careful! What happened years ago might suddenly become incredibly interesting and change the way you think!

Contents

Friends Across the Sea

The Declaration of Independence officially separated the 13 colonies from Great Britain's rule.

On July 4, 1776, 13 American colonies declared their independence from Great Britain. This Declaration of Independence was an important milestone in the American Revolution. The French Marquis de Lafayette sailed to America in 1777 and joined the forces under General George Washington. Lafayette's support was a sign of the strong friendship between France and the Americans.

France officially joined the revolution as an American ally in 1778. This marked a turning point in the war. American and French troops, with help from the French navy, defeated the British at the Battle of Yorktown in 1781. It was the war's last major conflict. The former British colonies became an independent nation in 1783. The United States of America was born.

The French greatly admired their American allies' fight for independence. But France was still a **monarchy**. The French Revolution erupted in 1789. Revolutionaries shouted the slogan "Liberty, equality, fraternity" as they overthrew the monarchy. France became a **republic**. But the new government was unstable and soon collapsed.

The French people looked to the young United States with a sense of hope. The United States represented freedom from oppressive rulers. The French dreamed of securing such freedom in their own troubled nation.

The French Revolution took place just a few years after the end of the American Revolution.

CHAPTER 1

A TRIBUTE TO LIBERTY

Bartholdi first got the idea for the Statue of Liberty in 1865.

ON A SUMMER EVENING IN 1865, a group of friends gathered for dinner near the city of Versailles in France. The host of the dinner party was a college professor named Édouard René Lefebvre de Laboulaye. He greatly admired the United States. A rising young sculptor named Frédéric-Auguste Bartholdi was among Laboulaye's guests that evening. Bartholdi wrote years later that Laboulaye told his guests he would like the French people to make a gift to the people of America. The gift would be a magnificent statue representing liberty.

Laboulaye had a great deal of respect for the United States.

A Dream of Democracy

Laboulaye was the author of a three-volume book on the history of the United States. He never once visited the United States. But he was an expert on its laws and government. Laboulaye had carefully followed the events of the Civil War. He celebrated the Union victory and the end of slavery. He mourned with the American people when President Abraham Lincoln was assassinated.

France was under the rule of Emperor Napoléon III when Laboulaye first spoke of a gift to the United States. Laboulaye and many other French people wanted a **democracy** established in France instead of being ruled by an emperor. They looked toward the successful government of the United States as a model.

Laboulaye had two important reasons for wanting the French people to give a statue to the United States. He believed that the statue would be a symbol of the lasting friendship between the two nations and show France's

The Museum of French History is located in the former Palace of Versailles in Paris, France. Its vast collections include documents, pictures, and statues that tell the story of France from its beginnings to the 20th century. See page 60 for a link to learn more about the museum.

respect for American democracy. He also wanted to send a message to French rulers that the French people had a deep love of liberty.

Napoléon III was a strict ruler who believed in the importance of military power.

The Lessons of War

Frédéric-Auguste Bartholdi was intrigued with the idea of building a statue as a gift to the United States. But such a project would be vastly expensive. No money was available. Bartholdi moved on to other ideas.

During the 1860s, work was under way on a canal across the **Isthmus** of Suez in Egypt. The Suez Canal was a shortcut for shipping. It would be a link between Europe and Asia. In 1867, Bartholdi approached the Egyptian ruler, or khedive, Ismail Pasha. He offered to build a huge statue in honor of the canal. The statue would be called "Progress: Egypt Carrying the Light to Asia."

Bartholdi created many sculptures during his career.

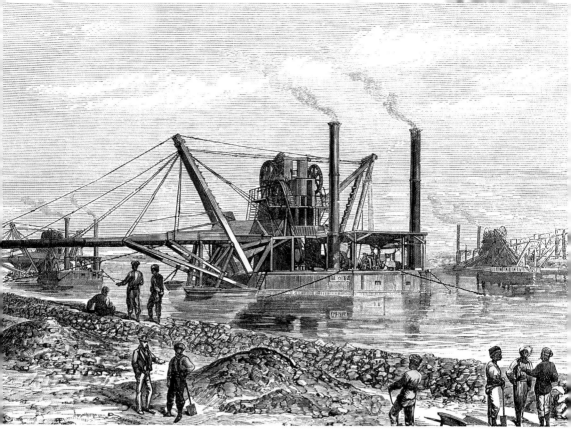

The Suez Canal was a major construction project that took 10 years to complete.

The khedive seemed interested. Bartholdi made a series of sketches and small **maquettes** of the monument he hoped to build. He envisioned the monument as a lady with a torch. The lady was draped in long, flowing robes. In some models, she held the torch in her right hand. In others, she carried it in her left. In a few, she wore a headdress that contained a lantern. Ismail Pasha encouraged Bartholdi's efforts but never offered him a **commission** to build the monument. Bartholdi finally abandoned the project.

In the summer of 1870, France declared war on Prussia, which today is part of Germany. Early in

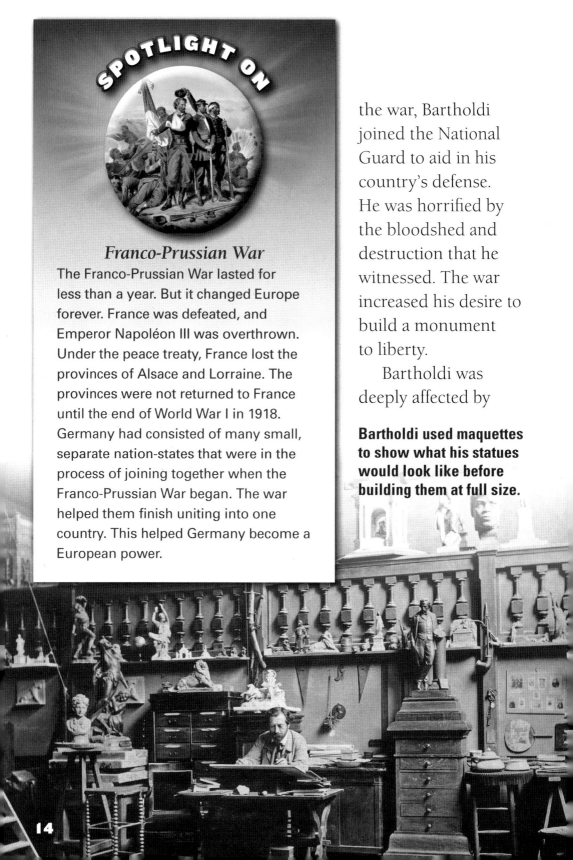

SPOTLIGHT ON

Franco-Prussian War

The Franco-Prussian War lasted for less than a year. But it changed Europe forever. France was defeated, and Emperor Napoléon III was overthrown. Under the peace treaty, France lost the provinces of Alsace and Lorraine. The provinces were not returned to France until the end of World War I in 1918. Germany had consisted of many small, separate nation-states that were in the process of joining together when the Franco-Prussian War began. The war helped them finish uniting into one country. This helped Germany become a European power.

the war, Bartholdi joined the National Guard to aid in his country's defense. He was horrified by the bloodshed and destruction that he witnessed. The war increased his desire to build a monument to liberty.

Bartholdi was deeply affected by

Bartholdi used maquettes to show what his statues would look like before building them at full size.

Paris suffered major damage during the Franco-Prussian War.

the war. Paris had been looted and burned. Bartholdi created many monuments and memorials to French heroes in the years after the war. His most famous monument was *The Lion of Belfort*. It was a huge stone lion carved into a cliff. The lion represented the strength of French troops who resisted the Prussians during a long siege of the city of Belfort.

The Franco-Prussian War inspired Bartholdi to create *The Lion of Belfort*.

A Trip to America

During the last months of the Franco-Prussian War, Bartholdi and Laboulaye again discussed the idea of a statue for the United States. They knew that the people of France were in no mood to raise money for such a project. But Laboulaye encouraged Bartholdi to move ahead with plans for the statue. Years later, Bartholdi wrote that Laboulaye advised him, "Go to America, study it, bring back your impressions. Propose to our friends over there to make with us a monument, a common work, in remembrance of the ancient friendship of France and the United States." Laboulaye gave Bartholdi letters of introduction to some of his many important friends across the Atlantic.

Bartholdi sailed to New York in the spring of 1871. He saw the perfect setting for the great statue as his ship glided into New York Harbor, "where people get their first view of the New World," he wrote. He called it "an admirable spot. It is Bedloe's Island, in the middle of the bay."

Laboulaye's letters of introduction helped Bartholdi meet some of the most powerful people in the United States. He spoke with Senators Charles Sumner and Carl

Frédéric-Auguste Bartholdi

Frédéric-Auguste Bartholdi (1834–1904) was born in the French province of Alsace, not far from today's border with Germany. When he was a child, his mother noticed that he had unusual artistic ability. She encouraged him to study drawing and sculpture. Bartholdi saw the Sphinx and other huge Egyptian statues on a tour of the Nile when he was a young man. He became fascinated with what was called monumental sculpture. He created many statues of French patriots and heroes. The Statue of Liberty was the greatest work of his life.

Bartholdi met with President Grant (right) during his trip to the United States.

Schurz. He met newspaper publishers, artists, writers, and architects. He even enjoyed a visit with President Ulysses S. Grant and his family.

Bartholdi boarded a train and headed west after exploring the East Coast from Washington to Boston. He saw vast bison herds and the smoke from Native American campfires as he crossed the Great Plains. In California, he was awed by the majesty of the great redwood trees. A mighty monument seemed fitting for a nation that grew trees so large!

Everywhere he went, Bartholdi talked about the statue he hoped to build. People listened politely. But the idea did not stir up much enthusiasm. The United States was recovering from the Civil War. Much of the country was still new and raw. Americans needed roads, telegraph lines, and schools. People could not muster much excitement for a monument to liberty, even if it came as a gift.

Bartholdi was not discouraged. When he sailed back to France, he was more determined than ever to build his statue. But he knew that an enormous task lay before him. He wrote to his mother, "[This] is sure to be a long and laborious process."

Bartholdi witnessed the damage from the Civil War firsthand.

CHAPTER 2
THE IDEA TAKES SHAPE

The Centennial
Exhibition was
scheduled to
take place at
Independence Hall
in Philadelphia,
Pennsylvania.

20

BARTHOLDI ESPECIALLY ENJOYED his tour of Philadelphia, Pennsylvania, during his visit to the United States in 1871. He was thrilled to stand in Independence Hall, where the members of the Continental Congress signed the Declaration of Independence. Philadelphians told him proudly that a great celebration would take place in 1876 to mark the 100th anniversary of the signing. Philadelphia would host a splendid fair called the Centennial **Exhibition**. What better way to honor the first century of the young nation, Bartholdi thought, than to present the United States with a magnificent statue?

The Early Models

Bartholdi began to shape his ideas for the liberty statue into clay models even before he set out for the United States. He drew upon his earlier design for "Egypt Carrying the Light to Asia." Bartholdi had designed the Suez Canal statue as a woman with a torch. He decided that a similar figure could represent liberty to the people of the United States.

Bartholdi created several female figures about 4 feet (1.2 meters) in height while working in his Paris studio. The figure's body was turned slightly in most of these early models. One arm

Today, Bartholdi's early models for the Statue of Liberty are located in museums.

swung by its side. Like several of his models for the Egyptian statue, these figures held an upraised torch. But Bartholdi added a new element in some of his models. A broken chain lay beneath the models' feet. The trampled chain had been used as a symbol by the antislavery movement in the United States during the 1850s.

Statues and paintings commonly represented liberty during the 19th century. Bartholdi carefully studied European and American liberty figures as his own ideas evolved. Liberty was often shown as a woman holding a sword and shield to symbolize victory over oppression. Some liberty figures carried a broken chain in one hand. Another symbol common to many liberty figures was the Roman **liberty cap**. This round, pointed cap was given to

Sculptor's Models

The creation of a monumental sculpture is a long process with many stages. The sculptor usually begins by making small clay models of the statue. The models help the artist decide on the statue's form and pose. Next the sculptor builds larger models. These might be twice the size of the earlier ones. The clay models may be cast in plaster to make them more durable. Once the form of the monument is determined, the artist begins the work of building on a large scale. Large monuments are usually built as separate pieces that are finally assembled on a **pedestal**.

newly freed slaves in ancient Rome. One of Bartholdi's early models for the liberty statue wore such a cap that had spaces through which a beacon light could shine.

Bartholdi made another clay model of the liberty statue while he was in New York in 1871. This model wore a sunburst instead of a liberty cap. This crown of

The Roman liberty cap was an important symbol of freedom during the French Revolution.

Vive la Nation

The Colossus at Rhodes, one of the Seven Wonders, may have been large enough for ships to sail between its legs.

seven rays symbolized the idea that the United States brought the light of liberty to the world.

Looking to the Past

Bartholdi learned everything he could about the massive artworks of the ancient world. The ancient Greeks had described major works of architecture and sculpture known as the Seven Wonders. Bartholdi was fascinated by accounts of one of the Seven Wonders, the Colossus at Rhodes. The Colossus was an enormous bronze figure

SPOTLIGHT ON

The Seven Wonders

The ancient Greeks and Romans compiled several lists of buildings and sculptures that they called the Seven Wonders. Here is the list that is most widely accepted today.

1. **The Pyramids of Giza, Egypt—** A group of three pyramids built near the present-day city of Cairo. The Pyramids are the only Wonder that survives today.
2. **The Hanging Gardens of Babylon—** Gardens built on terraces south of today's Baghdad, Iraq.
3. **Statue of Zeus at Olympia—** A 40-foot (12 m) gold and ivory statue that stood in ancient Greece.
4. **Temple of Artemis at Ephesus—** A columned marble temple in present-day Turkey.
5. **Mausoleum at Halicarnassus—** A tomb built for a king in today's Turkey.
6. **Colossus at Rhodes—**A bronze statue of the Greek god Helios.
7. **Pharos of Alexandria—**A lighthouse on an island off the Egyptian coast.

that overlooked the harbor on the island of Rhodes. It was completed in about 280 BCE and stood some 110 feet (33.5 m) high on a 50-foot (15 m) pedestal.

The Colossus represented Helios, the Greek god of the sun. According to some scholars, the statue wore a spiked crown to suggest the sun's rays. Legends claim that its legs spanned the harbor and that ships sailed between them. Most scholars doubt that this was the case.

In several ways, the Colossus resembled the statue that Bartholdi planned to build. It wore a sunburst crown, it overlooked a busy harbor, and it was very large. It was also dedicated to liberty. Reading and thinking about the Colossus at Rhodes had a strong influence on Bartholdi.

The Final Form

By 1872, Bartholdi had determined the pose that the statue would take. In his last models, the figure faced forward to give a sense of steadiness. The pose was relaxed, with the right leg slightly back. The graceful flow of the robes also suggested calm. The torch was lifted high in the statue's right hand.

A smaller version of the statue's final design is located in Paris.

The face of the statue was calm and dignified. No one knows for sure who served as Bartholdi's model. According to one story, he worked from his memory of a lovely young girl whom he saw killed during the

Bartholdi Park is named for its fountain's creator.

Franco-Prussian War. Some critics think that Bartholdi's wife served as his model. Still others believe that the model was his mother. Bartholdi may actually have

A FIRSTHAND LOOK AT
THE BARTHOLDI FOUNTAIN

Bartholdi also worked on other projects while he was designing the Statue of Liberty. He created a beautiful fountain for the 1876 Centennial Exhibition in Philadelphia. The fountain is now located in Bartholdi Park in Washington, D.C. See page 60 for a link to find out how you can visit the Bartholdi Fountain.

combined elements of several faces as he sculpted the face of the statue.

Laboulaye studied the evolving models with enthusiasm. He made an important suggestion as the statue neared its final form. He believed that the statue should hold a tablet representing the law in its left hand. Bartholdi agreed. He placed a tablet in the statue's left hand. On it was inscribed the date that the Declaration of Independence was issued. The date appeared in Roman numerals as "July IV, MDCCLXXVI."

The Statue of Liberty's tablet bears the date the Declaration of Independence became official.

CHAPTER 3

THE PROJECT MOVES FORWARD

Laboulaye used his influence in the National Assembly to get the liberty statue project approved.

Bartholdi hoped the statue would be completed in time for the 1876 centennial celebrations in the United States. But Laboulaye believed that the project had to wait until France became more stable. France had struggled to establish a new democratic government in the years after the war. Laboulaye was elected to the National Assembly. He helped write France's new constitution. In 1875, he finally thought that the time was right for the statue project to get under way.

The Franco-American Union explained that the statue would honor the French soldiers who had helped the United States win independence during the Revolutionary War (shown above).

The Franco-American Union

Laboulaye brought together a group of prominent French citizens and friends from the United States living in France in September 1875. The group was called the Franco-American Union. Laboulaye was chosen to serve as its president. The group's main purpose was to raise money to build the liberty statue.

A notice appeared in newspapers all over France shortly after the Union's founding. It announced that the Franco-American Union would be raising money to build a huge statue as a gift to the United States.

The notice explained that the statue would be built in memory of the French soldiers who fought for liberty in the American Revolution. It would also honor the connection between American independence and the new French republic. The statue would be called "Liberty Enlightening the World."

Laboulaye also wrote to other friends in the United States to win support for the statue project. He proposed that the French people would pay for the statue to be built and shipped across the Atlantic. The United States would provide a pedestal upon which the statue could stand. Laboulaye wrote to President Grant and asked him to designate Bedloe's Island as a site for the statue. Grant officially set aside Bedloe's Island for the statue on his last day in office in March 1877.

A certificate from the Franco-American Union gave Bartholdi permission to begin constructing the statue.

The People Respond

The Franco-American Union's newspaper notices stated that even the smallest donation would help the liberty statue project. Many ordinary citizens sent what they could afford.

The Union put most of its energy toward raising donations from the wealthy. The fund-raising effort opened with a party for 200 people at the Hotel du Louvre in Paris. Bartholdi's design for the statue was on display for the first time. It brought the project to life for the guests.

The Hotel du Louvre was the site of a major fund-raiser for the statue.

Gounod became a world-famous composer in the mid-1800s.

One of the most spectacular fund-raising events was a performance at the Paris Opera. Laboulaye delivered a stirring speech in which he explained that the statue was a tribute to liberty and peace. His speech was followed by the world's first performance of a musical composition by Charles-François Gounod. Gounod had composed the piece in honor of the statue.

Laboulaye was a powerful speaker. He was highly effective in winning support. He seized every opportunity to speak about the statue project. One observer wrote that he "gradually unlocked their hearts till he had the whole house on his side."

SPOTLIGHT ON

Repoussé

The sculpture technique called repoussé dates back to ancient Greece. Some scholars think it was used to build the Colossus at Rhodes. Repoussé required a full-size version of the statue to be made in plaster. Large wooden molds were then made to fit over each section of the plaster model. A sheet of copper was heated until it became soft enough to bend easily. The copper sheet was then hammered into a wooden mold until it took the mold's exact form. The copper held the shape of the mold when it cooled. Hundreds of hammered copper sheets could be joined together to form the outer layer of a statue.

The Challenge of Construction

Bartholdi moved ahead with his plans even before the funds began to flow in. He visited a Paris metal **foundry** called Gaget, Gauthier & Company. He asked which metal would be best for a monumental statue. Emile Gaget and J. G. Gauthier recommended copper. Copper could be formed into thin, lightweight sheets. These sheets could be hammered into any shape using an ancient process called ***repoussé***.

The thin copper shell of the statue could not stand on its own. Bartholdi thought long and hard about the interior of the statue. He consulted with a highly respected Paris architect named Eugène-Emmanuel Viollet-le-Duc. Viollet-le-Duc agreed to work with him. He suggested building an inner layer of copper. Sand would fill the space between the outer skin and the inner structure to make the statue stable.

Work on the statue got under way early in 1876. Bartholdi was at the foundry every day to oversee the workers. Each step of the long process had to be done perfectly. Bartholdi made sure that every detail of his design would appear in the final version of the statue.

The statue caught the attention of passersby as it grew larger and larger at the foundry.

A Public Preview

The statue was far from complete when the United States celebrated its centennial in the summer of 1876. But the American public had a chance to see the work in progress. An enormous painting of the Statue of Liberty by artist Jean-Baptiste Lavastre was on display in New York's

The Centennial Exhibition drew huge crowds of people from around the country.

Madison Square Garden. The painting gave the public an idea of what the finished statue would look like.

The statue's forearm, with the hand grasping the torch, was set up two months later at the Centennial Exhibition in Philadelphia. Thousands of visitors climbed the spiral ladder inside the arm and stepped onto the balcony that

A FIRSTHAND LOOK AT
THE CENTENNIAL EXHIBITION

Philadelphia's Centennial Exhibition in 1876 was a celebration unlike any the United States had ever seen. New inventions, agricultural methods, scientific discoveries, and works of art were on display. See page 60 for a link to see illustrations of the exhibition online.

surrounded the torch's copper flame. This gave them an idea of the size of the statue that was being constructed in France. The American public began to look forward to the completion of the statue.

The arm and torch on display at the Centennial Exhibition began to generate excitement for the statue's completion.

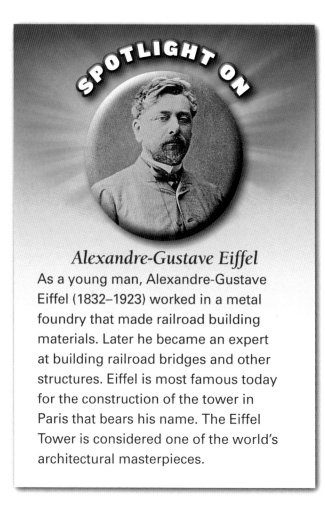

Alexandre-Gustave Eiffel

As a young man, Alexandre-Gustave Eiffel (1832–1923) worked in a metal foundry that made railroad building materials. Later he became an expert at building railroad bridges and other structures. Eiffel is most famous today for the construction of the tower in Paris that bears his name. The Eiffel Tower is considered one of the world's architectural masterpieces.

The Final Phase

Viollet-le-Duc died suddenly in September 1879. Only the upper portions of the statue were complete. Bartholdi hired skilled architect Alexandre-Gustave Eiffel to finish the internal structure. Eiffel had his own ideas for supporting the statue. He recommended building a massive iron column instead of using an inner shell and a layer of sand. The 98-foot (30 m) column would stand inside the statue and extend into the right arm. Work on Eiffel's column began in 1881.

Gaget and Gauthier hammered out the last sections of the statue's copper skin as Eiffel and his crew worked on the supporting tower. Bartholdi decided to assemble the entire statue in a yard beside the foundry. The right arm and torch were shipped back to France for the statue's final assembly. Every day, hundreds of people streamed past the yard to watch the statue rise, piece by piece, toward the sky.

The Franco-American Union presented *Liberty Enlightening the World* to the United States' minister to France at a ceremony on July 4, 1884. The copper figure towered 151 feet (46 m) over the narrow Paris street. The day was both happy and sad for Bartholdi. His longtime friend and supporter, Laboulaye, would never see the statue completed. Laboulaye had died in 1883 at the age of 72.

Photographs were taken of the statue as it was constructed.

CHAPTER 4

LIBERTY ENLIGHTENING THE WORLD

The statue needed a pedestal to stand on before it could be sent to the United States.

THE STATUE OF LIBERTY WAS a gift from the people of France. But a large share of the responsibility for the statue fell to the people of the United States. They had to clear Bedloe's Island and prepare the site for the statue. They also had to provide the statue's pedestal. A group of politicians, business owners, and newspaper publishers formed the American Committee in the fall of 1876. Its purpose was to raise money to build a pedestal for the statue from France.

American Contributions

The American Committee asked architects to submit their ideas for the statue's pedestal. Architect Richard Morris Hunt submitted the winning design. He proposed to build a granite tower 180 feet (55 m) in height. The committee later decided that this design would be too costly to build. Hunt submitted several other plans. The committee accepted a design consisting of a three-level, square tower 89 feet (27 m) high.

Work at Bedloe's Island began in April 1883. Workers dug a square hole 15 feet (4.6 m) deep and 91 feet long

Hunt designed a pedestal that is more than half as tall as the statue itself.

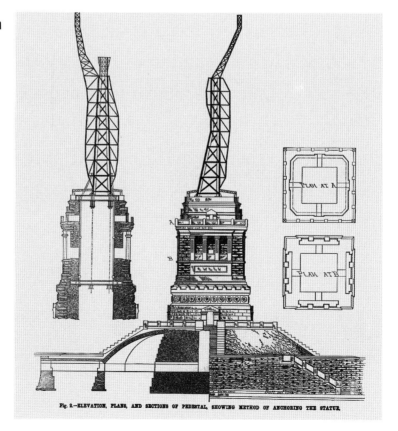

Fig. 2.—ELEVATION, PLANS, AND SECTIONS OF PEDESTAL, SHOWING METHOD OF ANCHORING THE STATUE.

The base needed to be strong enough to support the heavy statue that would sit on top of it.

(28 m) on each side for the **foundation**. The massive base for the pedestal was set within the foundation.

Fund-raising went slowly at first. Americans did not want to pay for the pedestal. A writer in *Harper's Magazine* commented, "We catch ourselves . . . wishing that M. Bartholdi and our French cousins had 'gone the whole figure' while they were about it, and given us

TODAY'S PERSPECTIVE

Emma Lazarus's poem was nearly forgotten for 20 years. But today, it is an important part of the Statue of Liberty. In 1903, one of Lazarus's admirers had it inscribed on a plaque. The plaque was displayed on the second level of the statue's pedestal. The poem became popular during the 1930s and 1940s. The plaque was moved to the entrance hall of the pedestal in 1945. The poem ends with the famous lines, "Give me your tired, your poor, / Your huddled masses yearning to breathe free, / The wretched refuse of your teeming shore. / Send these, the homeless, tempest-tost to me, / I lift my lamp beside the golden door!"

statue and pedestal at once." The committee increased its efforts. It raised money by holding concerts, plays, dances, and art exhibitions.

The People's Statue

In 1883, the American Committee asked a young New York poet named Emma Lazarus to write a poem about the statue. Her poem, "The New Colossus," appeared in the brochure for an art auction. The auction was held to raise funds for the statue's pedestal.

Despite the efforts of the American Committee, funds petered out in the fall of 1884. Work on the pedestal ground to a halt. Newspaper publisher Joseph Pulitzer launched a fund-raising campaign in March 1885. In the pages of his newspaper, he urged the American people to help fund the project. More than 120,000 people sent in donations.

Some donations were large. But most amounts were under a dollar. Even American children contributed to the statue project. Thousands of children sent nickels and pennies to Pulitzer's fund. By August, he had raised $100,000. Work on the pedestal resumed.

The Statue Comes Ashore

Across the Atlantic, crews of workers disassembled the statue in the yard beside the foundry. Each piece of the copper skin and each section of the support tower were carefully labeled. The statue was at last loaded aboard the French warship *Isère*. It was packed in more than 200 crates and weighed a total of 150 tons.

One fund-raising campaign promised miniature versions of the statue in return for donations.

Statue of "Liberty Enlightening the World."

The Committee in charge of the construction of the base and pedestal for the reception of this great work, **in order to raise funds for its completion,** have prepared a miniature Statuette *six inches in height*—the Statue Bronzed; Pedestal, Nickel-silvered —which they are now delivering to subscribers throughout the United States at **One Dollar Each.**

This attractive souvenir and Mantel or Desk ornament is a *perfect fac-simile* of the model furnished by the artist. The Statuette in same metal, *twelve inches high*, at **Five Dollars Each,** delivered.

The designs of Statue and Pedestal are protected by U. S. Patents, and the models can *only* be furnished by this Committee. Address, with remittance,

RICHARD BUTLER
American Committee of the S

YESTERDAY'S HEADLINES

Joseph Pulitzer (above) used powerful tactics of persuasion to get people to donate to the statue pedestal fund. He emphasized that the statue belonged to the American people. It was up to the American people to see that the pedestal was built. In one column, he told his readers, "Let us not wait for the millionaires to give this money. It is not a gift from the millionaires of France to the millionaires of America, but a gift of the whole people of France to the whole people of America."

The *Isère* landed at Bedloe's Island on June 17, 1885. Workers were busy finishing the pedestal as the giant crates were unloaded. Not until the summer of 1886 could the process of reassembling the statue get under way. Crowds gathered every day to watch the workers as they fastened the pieces into place.

The Grand Dedication

A parade made its way through the streets of Manhattan on October 28, 1886. Bands played, crowds cheered, and flags rippled in the breeze. Schools and businesses were closed for the great occasion of the dedication of the statue. According to

A parade made its way through the streets of New York City on the way to the dedication of the Statue of Liberty.

some reports, as many as one million people lined the sidewalks.

A veil was removed from the great statue's face early in the afternoon. The Statue of Liberty towered above

A VIEW FROM ABROAD

News stories about the dedication of the Statue of Liberty appeared in papers around the world. People all over the globe saw the statue as a tribute to freedom and a symbol of hope. The Cuban journalist José Martí wrote that the statue represented the struggle of oppressed peoples such as the Irish, Poles, Italians, Czechs, Alsatians, and many more. He also mentioned the oppression of African Americans who, though freed from slavery, did not yet enjoy liberty in their own nation.

People came from all around to attend the statue's dedication.

the harbor. It stood taller than any building in New York City. On that October afternoon, it was the tallest structure in the United States.

President Grover Cleveland spoke to the crowd. He thanked the

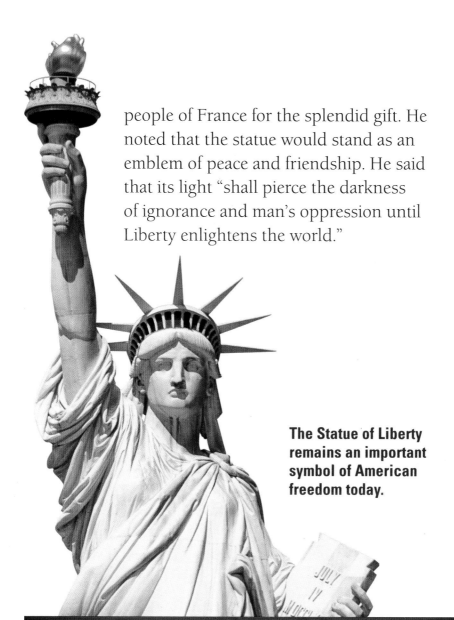

people of France for the splendid gift. He noted that the statue would stand as an emblem of peace and friendship. He said that its light "shall pierce the darkness of ignorance and man's oppression until Liberty enlightens the world."

The Statue of Liberty remains an important symbol of American freedom today.

A FIRSTHAND LOOK AT
THE STATUE OF LIBERTY

The Statue of Liberty stands on Liberty Island (formerly called Bedloe's Island) in New York Harbor. Visitors may enter the pedestal and climb to the statue's crown. See page 60 to learn how you can visit the statue.

What Happened Where?

Newark Bay

Bayonne

Staten Island

N
W E
S

0   0.5   1 mi

0   0.5   1 km

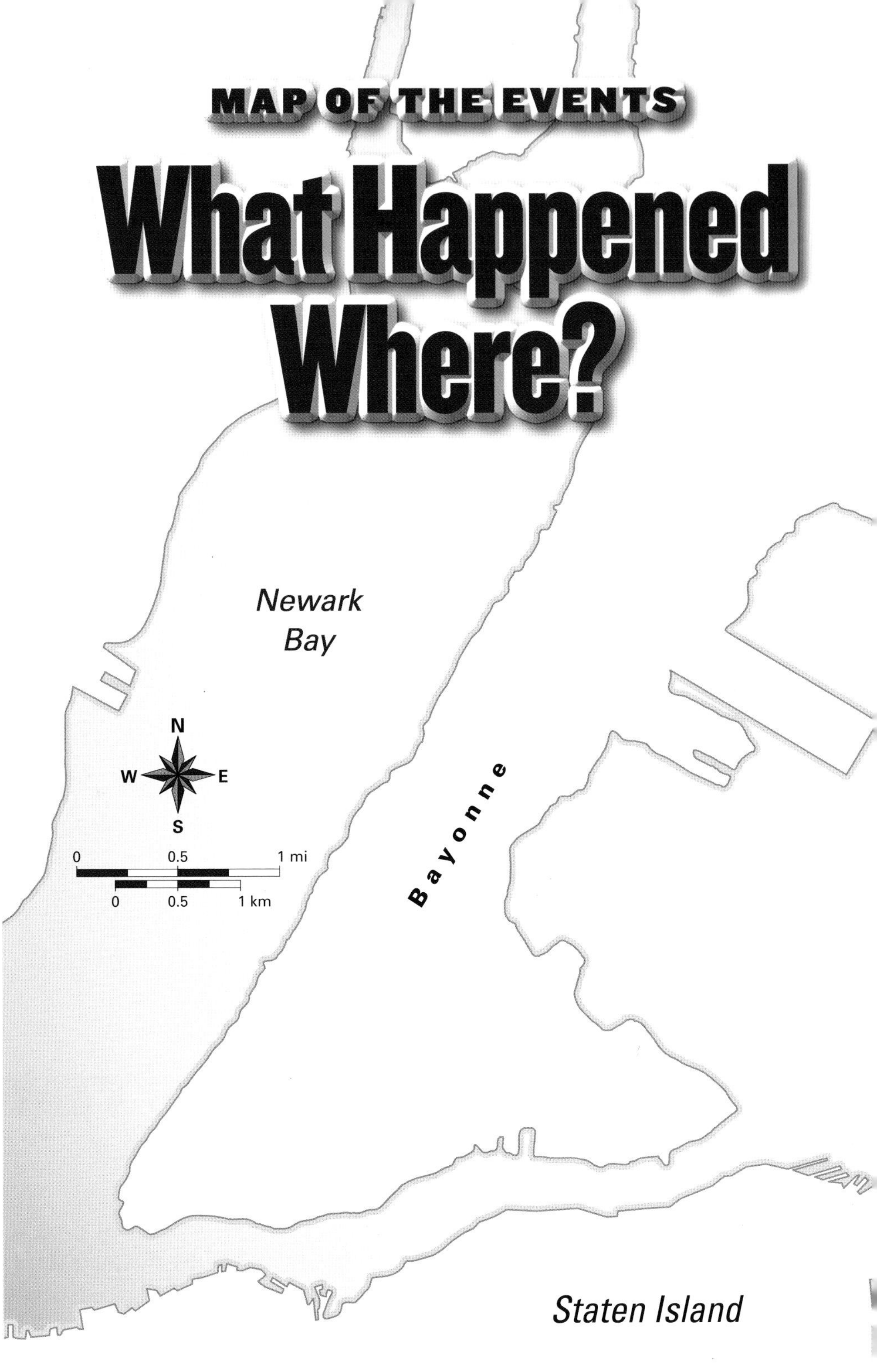

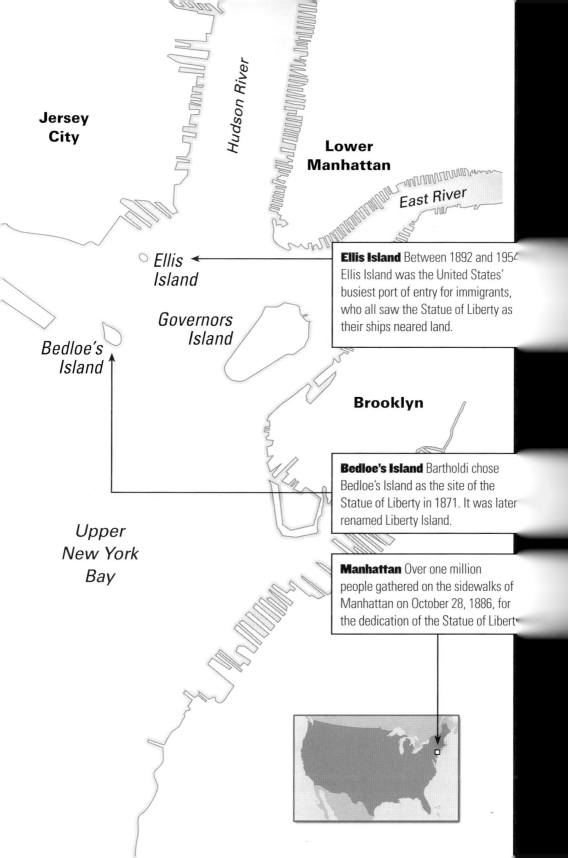

Jersey City

Hudson River

Lower Manhattan

East River

○ *Ellis Island*

Governors Island

Bedloe's Island

Brooklyn

Upper New York Bay

Ellis Island Between 1892 and 195⌐ Ellis Island was the United States' busiest port of entry for immigrants, who all saw the Statue of Liberty as their ships neared land.

Bedloe's Island Bartholdi chose Bedloe's Island as the site of the Statue of Liberty in 1871. It was later renamed Liberty Island.

Manhattan Over one million people gathered on the sidewalks of Manhattan on October 28, 1886, for the dedication of the Statue of Libert⌐

A Symbol of Welcome

A 1936 ceremony honored the statue's 50th anniversary.

Management of the Statue of Liberty has changed several times. The U.S. Lighthouse Board was in charge of the statue in the early years. The War Department became responsible for its maintenance in 1901. A presidential proclamation made the statue a national monument in 1924. The statue's care was transferred to the National Park Service in 1933. The name Bedloe's Island was changed to Liberty Island in 1956. Neighboring Ellis

Island was also placed under the National Park Service in 1965. That year, the two islands became the Statue of Liberty National Monument.

The Statue of Liberty is often battered by storms and saltwater spray. It eventually began to show its age. President Ronald Reagan authorized a full-scale restoration project in 1982. The statue was closed for renovation from January 23, 1984, until July 5, 1986.

The Statue of Liberty was also closed to visitors after the terrorist attacks on the World Trade Center and the Pentagon on September 11, 2001. Visitors were permitted to enter the pedestal in 2004. Visitors were once again free to climb to the statue's crown in 2007.

Today, the Statue of Liberty is revered throughout the world. Its torch held high, it signals a generous welcome to all.

A worker takes a break during the 1980s restoration of the statue.

O VISIT THE STATUE OF LIBERTY EACH DAY

Édouard René Lefebvre de Laboulaye

Marie-Joseph-Paul-Yves-Roch-Gilbert du Motier, Marquis de Lafayette (1757–1834)
was a French nobleman who volunteered to help the colonial forces during the American Revolution. At the age of 19, he was commissioned a major general. His assistance strengthened the friendship between France and the United States.

Édouard René Lefebvre de Laboulaye
(1811–1883) was a French scholar and political leader with a passionate belief in individual freedom. He never visited the United States, but he was an expert on U.S. history. He envisioned the gift of a statue representing liberty for the American people and worked to raise money for its completion.

Eugène-Emmanuel Viollet-le-Duc
(1814–1879) was a French architect noted for his restorations of buildings from the Middle Ages. He earned fame for his work on the Cathedral of Notre-Dame in Paris. He was in charge of building a supporting structure for the Statue of Liberty but died before the work was completed.

Charles-François Gounod (1818–1893) was
a French composer of operas, symphonies, and sacred music. His song "La Liberté éclairant le monde" was composed for a performance to raise money for the statue project. The song was not published until 1894.

Richard Morris Hunt (1827–1895) was an American architect who built the pedestal for the Statue of Liberty. He studied architecture in Paris. His work combines elements of European and American architectural styles.

Alexandre-Gustave Eiffel (1832–1923) was a French engineer and architect. He launched his career as a builder of bridges. He designed the column that supports the Statue of Liberty from within. He is best known for his creation of the Eiffel Tower, which he completed for the 1889 International Exposition in Paris.

Frédéric-Auguste Bartholdi

Frédéric-Auguste Bartholdi (1834–1904) was a French sculptor known for his large memorials and monuments. In addition to the Statue of Liberty, he created a statue of the Marquis de Lafayette that stands in New York City.

Joseph Pulitzer (1847–1911) was an American journalist and publisher. Born in Hungary, he moved to the United States to serve in the Civil War. As publisher of the *New York World*, he helped raise money to build the pedestal for the Statue of Liberty. The Pulitzer Prizes—important awards given to journalists, authors, photographers, and composers—are named in his honor.

Joseph Pulitzer

Emma Lazarus (1849–1887) was an American poet. Raised in New York City and Newport, Rhode Island, she belonged to a prosperous Jewish family. She published a novel and several collections of poetry. Her best-known poem, "The New Colossus," can be read on a plaque near the entrance to the Statue of Liberty.

TIMELINE

1865

Édouard René Lefebvre de Laboulaye suggests the idea for the gift of a statue from the French people to the people of the United States.

1867

Sculptor Frédéric-Auguste Bartholdi plans the giant statue of a woman with a torch for the opening of the Suez Canal in Egypt.

1871

Bartholdi visits the United States to find a location for the statue.

1883

Poet Emma Lazarus writes "The New Colossus" in honor of the statue.

1884

July 4
Assembly of the statue is completed in Paris; the statue is presented to the U.S. minister to France as a gift to the American people.

1885

June 17
The French warship *Isère* reaches Bedloe's Island with the disassembled statue on board.

1933

The National Park Service becomes responsible for managing the Statue of Liberty.

1956

Bedloe's Island is renamed Liberty Island.

1965

Liberty Island and Ellis Island become the Statue of Liberty National Monument.

1875
Laboulaye establishes the Franco-American Union to raise money to build the statue.

1876
The arm of the statue, holding the torch, is displayed at the Centennial Exhibition in Philadelphia; the American Committee is formed to raise money for the statue's pedestal.

1877
U.S. president Ulysses S. Grant sets aside Bedloe's Island as the site for the statue.

1886
October 28
The Statue of Liberty is dedicated in a ceremony.

1901
Management of the Statue of Liberty is placed under the War Department.

1924
The Statue of Liberty becomes a national monument.

1986
After two years of restoration, the Statue of Liberty is reopened to the public.

2001
The Statue of Liberty is closed after the attacks on the World Trade Center and Pentagon.

2007
The public is once more permitted to climb to the crown of the statue.

LIVING HISTORY

Primary sources provide firsthand evidence about a topic. Witnesses to a historical event create primary sources. They include autobiographies, newspaper reports of the time, oral histories, photographs, and memoirs. A secondary source analyzes primary sources, and is one step or more removed from the event. Secondary sources include textbooks, encyclopedias, and commentaries.

The Bartholdi Fountain Many of Bartholdi's works can be seen around the world today. A fountain he created for the 1876 Centennial Exhibition in Philadelphia is currently located in Washington, D.C.'s Bartholdi Park. To find out more about the fountain and how you can visit the park, visit *www.usbg.gov/gardens/bartholdi-park.cfm*

The Centennial Exhibition Philadelphia's Centennial Exhibition in 1876 was a celebration unlike any the United States had ever seen. New inventions, agricultural methods, scientific discoveries, and works of art were on display. To see illustrations of the fairgrounds, buildings, and displays, visit *www.bc.edu/bc_org/avp/cas/fnart /fa267/1876fair.html*

The Museum of French History The Museum of French History is home to many documents, pictures, and statues that help tell the story of France's history. This museum can help you understand what was going on in France at the time when the Statue of Liberty was being built. For a virtual tour or to find out how you can visit the museum in person, visit *http://en.chateauversailles.fr/discover-the -estate/the-palace/the-palace/museum-of-the-history-of-france*

The Statue of Liberty The Statue of Liberty on Liberty Island is one of the most frequently visited attractions in New York City. To enter the statue and climb to the crown, you will need to make a reservation in advance. Find out how you can go see the statue by visiting *www.nps.gov/stli/*

RESOURCES

Books

Behrens, Janice. *What Is the Statue of Liberty?* New York: Children's Press, 2009.

Glaser, Linda. *Emma's Poem: The Voice of the Statue of Liberty*. Boston: Houghton Mifflin, 2010.

Malam, John. *You Wouldn't Want to Be a Worker on the Statue of Liberty! A Monument You'd Rather Not Build*. New York: Franklin Watts, 2009.

Niz, Xavier. *The Story of the Statue of Liberty*. Mankato, MN: Capstone Press, 2006.

Rappaport, Doreen. *Lady Liberty: A Biography*. Cambridge, MA: Candlewick, 2008.

Shea, Pegi Deitz. *Liberty Rising: The Story of the Statue of Liberty*. New York: Henry Holt, 2005.

Web Sites

Statue of Liberty-Ellis Island Foundation
www.statueofliberty.org/
Learn about Ellis Island, which is part of the Statue of Liberty National Monument.

Statue of Liberty National Monument
www.nps.gov/stli
This is the official site of the National Park Service. It provides information about fees and reservations for visiting the statue and what you will see when you get there.

Visit this Scholastic Web site for more information on the Statue of Liberty:
www.factsfornow.scholastic.com

GLOSSARY

commission (kuh-MISH-uhn) an offer of money to do creative work, such as writing music or designing a building

democracy (di-MAH-kruh-see) a form of government in which people choose their leaders in elections

exhibition (ek-suh-BISH-uhn) a public display of things that interest people

foundation (foun-DAY-shuhn) a solid structure on which a building is constructed

foundry (FOUN-dree) a factory for melting and shaping metal

isthmus (IS-muhs) a narrow strip of land that lies between two bodies of water and connects two larger landmasses

liberty cap (LIB-ur-tee KAP) a round, pointed cap given to Roman slaves after they gained their freedom; it is sometimes used in art as a symbol of liberty

maquettes (mah-KEHTS) a sculptor's small models created during the planning of a larger statue

monarchy (MAH-nar-key) a government in which the head of state is a king or a queen

pedestal (PED-i-stuhl) the base of a statue

repoussé (reh-poo-SAY) a technique of hammering thin copper sheets into wooden molds to form sections of a monumental statue

republic (ri-PUHB-lik) a form of government in which the people have the power to elect representatives who manage the government

INDEX

Page numbers in *italics* indicate illustrations.

ABOUT THE AUTHOR

Deborah Kent is a graduate of Oberlin College. She also holds a master's degree from Smith College School for Social Work. Ms. Kent has written nearly two dozen young adult novels and two dozen nonfiction titles for younger readers. She lives in Chicago with her husband.